Working in Wigan Mills

One Hundred years of Photographs

John Hannavy & Chris Ryan

Smiths Books

Companions to this volume

Maypole: Diary of a Mining Disaster
John Hannavy & Roy Lewis
Pictures of Wigan: 1860-1920
John Hannavy
Wigan Pier: An Illustrated History
John Hannavy & Jack Winstanley
Living & Working in Wigan
John Hannavy & Chris Ryan
In preparation:
Only Yesterday Pictures of Wigan 1920-1960
John Hannavy & Jack Winstanley

Series Editor John Hannavy

cover illustration: Rylands Gidlow Mills, Warping Room c.1909
(John Hannavy Picture Collection)

Published by Smiths Books (Wigan) Ltd.,
41-45 Mesnes Street, Wigan. tel. 42810/46270

text © 1987 John Hannavy & Chris Ryan

Designed by Peter J Kneebone MSIAD

ISBN 0 9510680 2 4

printed by The Hallgate Press, Wigan.

Contents

Acknowledgements

The authors and publishers are, as usual, grateful to a considerable number of people and institutions for help, advice and particularly for the loan of pictures. Particular thanks are due to the Wigan Reporter who published our requests for information and pictures, and to the many readers of that newspaper who answered our call and supplied most of the photographs reproduced here.

For help and advice we are grateful to Bob Blakeman, Courtaulds plc, Dunn & Co, Robin Grayson, Arnold Taylor, and particularly Mairi Macleod who originally intended to collaborate on this project and when unable to do so, placed her research notes at our disposal.

For photographs, we record out thanks to Peter Blinston, F.E. Case, Mrs. Conner, John Cullen, Mrs. Alice Derbyshire, Mr. Eaborn, Mr. Foster, Mrs. Gee, Mrs. Holton, Lancashire Publications - with special thanks to Allan Rimmer News Editor, F. Little, Mrs. Margaret Matthews, Mrs. Louisa Shepherd, Mrs. Sixsmith, Sydney Smith, Mrs. M. Speakman, Mr. Windsor, Jack Winstanley, Vincent Waring and Wigan Record Office in Leigh, with special thanks to Alastair Gillies and Len Hudson. Thanks also to Terry Davies, Managing Director of Coops Ltd., and to Arthur Pimlott, Terry Simpson and Burt Sharrock of Dorma Ltd., who all helped us greatly by allowing us access to their premises to take original photographs. As neither of us had ever experienced what the inside of a weaving shed was like, the visit to Dorma at Eckersley Mill was a most valuable part of our researches.

Our wives, Eileen and Alison are, by this time, getting used to us retiring to the office for the evening, or rushing off at a few minutes' notice to track down new and exciting pictures. For their tolerance and patience with us, special thanks are due.

Finally, thanks as usual to Trevor Smith for his support and encouragement with this third title in the series to be published under the Smiths Book imprint.

John Hannavy & Chris Ryan April 1987.

Introduction

What we have set out to produce in compiling "Working in Wigan Mills" is by no stretch of the imagination a definitive history of Wigan's textile industry. We gladly leave that task - which certainly needs to be done - to authors much more qualified to complete it than us. This is essentially an album of photographs, covering the period between 1887 and 1987, coupled with a brief historical background against which to view the photographs themselves. The captions are a mixture of factual information and personal anecdotes from former mill workers - to all of whom we owe a debt of thanks for their time and their reminiscences.

Arthur Munby, whose concern for the lot of Wigan's pit brow lasses formed a substantial part of our last book. "Living & Working in Wigan" made only passing reference to the mill girls in the diaries of his visits to the town. Staying in the Royal Hotel at the top of Standishgate in September 1873, he remarked only that his sleep had been disturbed at 5.30 a.m. by the noise of the mill girls on their way to their work. "The broad street" he wrote, "was busy with women and girls, clogshoon and most of them with shawls on their heads, all tramping in groups of two or three, and talking broad Lancashire audibly."

He was very concerned about the pit lasses, but gave the mill girls only a few lines in his diary before he returned to bed and slept soundly until ten o'clock.

Munby had little interest in the 'factory girls' as he called them, save for a few remarks by way of comparing their lot with that of servants, pit lasses and other working women in whom he had much more interest.

The picture Munby painted of Wigan's workforce of women, therefore, was hardly complete. At the time he was writing - in the mid 1870s - textile industry in the town was centuries old and highly developed. In the 1869 trade directory, the first published for the town, nearly fifty companies were already well established, employing thousands of people, mainly women.

That trade directory lists twenty seven cotton spinning mills, seven cotton manufacturers, and nearly a dozen other companies involved in servicing the cotton mills -bobbin turners, spindle and fly makers, dyers, finishers and so on. Added to that number were many more companies involved in clothing manufacture - an aspect of Wigan's enployment portfolio which has developed and continued from that day to this.

Many of the mills, however, have long since ceased production. Indeed only one weaving shed still produces cotton in the town. The buildings themselves have either decayed, been demolished, or have been refurbished and put to a different use.

It is wrong, however, to assume that the town no longer has a textile industry - is has albeit on a vastly reduced scale.

Of the buildings which still stand, Rylands' Gidlow Mill has for a long time been used as a mail order warehouse by Great Universal Stores, and now looks forward to a new lease of life as part of Wigan College of Technology, housing a range of college departments fro building to art and design. The move of that latter depar ment into the building will at least restore some conta between the mill and the textile and clothing industry, the college has a strong teaching base in fashion and te tiles.

Trencherfield Mill is, at the time of writing, partly u ed by Courtaulds subsidiary Wm. Christy & Co. partly u ed by the College and partly under continuing developme as part of the museum complex which makes up the Wiga Pier development.

Eckersley's Swan Meadow Mills complex, one of th largest sites in the area, houses the Dorma productic complex, in addition to activities as diverse as small i dustrial units, a cooperative and roller disco. Again at t time of writing, part of the currently unused floors of th mill are being used as locations for the filming by La broke Films of a surreal drama about Shostakovitch. Pe

1. Rylands' Gidlow Mills. Built in 1867 and 1868, Rylands' Mill occupies a prime position overlooking Mesnes Park. Used as a mail order warehouse for the past few years, it now looks forward to a new lease of life as part of Wigan College of Technology.

yhurst Mill still stands in part at least, and part of
'aylor's Victoria Mills is currently used by the
mith/Shearings Coach Group, but few of the other mills
'hich made up a close-knit textile complex around the
anal basin have survived. Mills such as Rose Bridge Mills
n Ince, Dicconson Lane Mills in Aspull and others find
hemselves in use for a variety of service and manufactur-
ng functions.

While these pictures may not represent a totally lost
ndustry, they do evoke memories of a lost life style. The
ride with which the mill workers posed for photographs
t Coronations, at Christmas time, or just because they
'ere a group of friends who wished to be remembered
ogether - suggests a friendship, a happiness and a sense of
urpose which overcame the noise and atmosphere of the
'orking conditions. The people in these pictures - and
hose we have talked to while researching this book - were
ll proud to work in Wigan Mills. This book is a tribute to
hem and the industry they served and developed.

2. The original Statement of Cost for Gidlow Mills shows that the buildings themselves were erected for the princely sum of £140,968.15.0d. including gas works, machinery and associated works.

Statement of Cost — Buildings Engines Gearing Machinery &c. &c. at Gidlow Works Wigan. as per Invoices to April 1st 1868.

Mill.— Building	40,703 12 5			
Gearing	6,959 9 2			
Engines, Boilers &c.	6,936 1 2	54,599 2 9	
Machinery		29,873 10	
Shed.— Buildings	19,000			
Gearing	2,881 11 5			
Engines, Boilers &c.	2,429 5	26,310 16 5	
Machinery		5,883 15	
Chimney		822 9 10	
Warehouses & Offices (including Stone Pillars)		7,500	
Reservoir		7,439 4 7	
Gas Works		4,000	
Manager's House		1,400	
Bridge		1,317 3	
Store Rooms		922 10 2	
Railway Wall		900	
		£140,968 15 0	

— 18th Decr. 1868. —

by M. White

7

3. Rylands Mill. John Thomas Beesley was an overlooker in the weaving shed when this picture was taken about 1904. The Mill used cotton from Egypt, India and America, each cotton having quatities suitable for specific cloths. John Beesley left Rylands to work at Taylor's Mill in the 1920s.

Wigan's Cotton Industry

Although most of the remains of Wigan's textile industry date from the last century, the earliest records of textile manufacture in the town date the fourteenth century. There were three fulling mills in operation in Wigan in that period - Coppull Mill and the "Old Mill of Wigan" were both on the upper Douglas using the river as a source of power while another, Lorington Mill, was on Clarington Brook between Wigan and Ince. Fulling had been part of the finishing process for cloth since Roman times. It involved soaking the cloth in soapy water and trampling it underfoot to make it shrink and tighten the weave. The efficiency of the process improved in the thirteenth century by the use of fulling stocks. These were heavy hammers that pounded the cloth and were so large that they could only be driven by water power.

The existence of these mills indicates that the cloth industry was already well established in Wigan by that time, though much of the economic life of the town was centred on agriculture, with spinning and weaving carried out only as a part time activity. Gradually cloth production emerged as a craft in its own right. The first mention of weaving as an individual occupation in the town, as far as can be ascertained, dates from 1601, and there was a spinner listed as operating in the town by 1629. These craftsmen would have handled wool, linen and fustian, a cloth with a linen warp and a cotton weft. The raw materials would have been bought by enterpreneurs in Manchester with trade connections in London, and then distributed via middlemen to the spinners and weavers in Wigan. At that time the town was also known as an important centre for the manufacture of bedding, but hardly any cotton cloth was made, and what little was produced was of poor quality.

In the second half of the eighteenth century, the cotton industry expanded out of all recognition, but only after ways had been found to replace skills that had taken years to acquire with machines which could be worked after only a short training. The growth of the industry was based on a rapid increase in the availability of raw cotton from America, and technological advances that produced Hargreaves' Spinning Jenny, Arkwright's Water Frame and Samuel Crompton's Mule. The industry took off in Lancashire and North Cheshire because the area enjoyed a number of advantages favourible to its development -Liverpool as a port for raw cotton imports, a damp climate ideal for spinning, an already established textile trade in woolens and linens, Manchester as a market for the finished cloth and, to become of increasing importance later especially in Wigan, an abundance of cheap coal.

The development of the cotton industry in Wigan in the last quarter of the eighteenth century is not well chronicled, especially relating to the transition from a home based industry to the large mills with which we are so familiar today. We know that in 1804 there were mills in Wigan working from 5 in the morning until 9 at night, and that they employed a number of children as young as eight years of age. Indeed they were so tired by nightfall that the overlookers beat them with leather straps to keep them awake.

In 1811, Samuel Crompton undertook a census of the cotton industry and found that in Wigan, of the twenty eight businesses he visited, the majority had capacities of less than 2,500 spindles, and only one had more than 10,000. The census confirms other evidence from that period that the town's mills were relatively small in comparison with other cotton towns - where mills were upwards of 25,000 spindles were not uncommon. In 1819 there were eight mills in Wigan employing a total of 616 people, with an average working day of fourteen hours. The vast majority were "Jenny Mills", with the machines operated by hand, and in which the manufacturing process had changed little over the preceding twenty years - and this at a time when mills in Manchester had boasted mules driven by steam engines since 1790. Lack of investment may have hampered the growth of the industry in Wigan in that period, with any surplus capital being invested in coal rather than in cotton. In the 1820s, however, the industry entered a new phase. The mills which were to dominate cotton production in the town until well into the twentieth century were all established at that time. Joseph Rylands and William Woods were already working in Wallgate in 1816, and Woods was soon to build the first Trencherfield Mills - in the 1820s, Eckersley's Swan Meadow Mill was

operating by 1822 and Thomas Taylor's first Victoria M by the mid 1830s.

The industrialisation of the Wigan district was given great impetus by the construction of the Leeds Liverpo Canal. By 1774, boats could sail from Liverpool to Wiga and in 1820 a branch was opened to Leigh, connecting wi the Bridgewater Canal and providing an alternative rou from Liverpool to Manchester by water. Liverpool ha replaced London as the main port for the cotton trade the 1790s and before the town was linked to the Liverpo -Manchester railway in 1832, the canals enjoyed a virtu monopoly in the transport of cotton. This fact encourage mill owners in the town to build their mills at the can side.

The early technological advances in the texti industry centred on the spinning process, so that with t vast increase in spun cotton, weaving became t bottleneck - but not for long. The power loom w invented in the1780s and it was gradually installed Lancashire mills in the first half of the nineteeth centur The mechanisation of weaving was a severe blow to t handloom weaver who was often head of a househol From being a relatively well paid craftsman still working home, the power loom made much of the weaver's sk obsolete and plunged many families into poverty. T misery was compounded by a process that was long a drawn out. The weavers organised a fullscale stri throughout Lancashire in 1808 to protest against falli wages and in Wigan weavers seized the shuttles out of t houses of those of their colleagues who were less keen joining the strike to prevent them from carrying working. In 1829 weavers in the town organised fo strikes and agreed not to buy milk and butter until pri were reduced. They were also apparently prepared resort to machine breaking. To counter this, Willia Woods - who had been the first to install powered looms Wigan at Trencherfield in the1820s - borrowed two canne from Lord Balcarres and stationed them at the entrance his mill to protect his new machines.

At about that time, Rylands employed some 2,0 handloom weavers, and both Woods and Eckersley h similar numbers working for them. The millowners ga out spun cotton to the weavers, who would then work it into finished cotton. According to the1851 census, the were still significant numbers of handloom weave working in the Scholes and Hardybutts areas, many

em Irish immigrants. Gradually, however, the numbers
clined and following the cotton famine of the early
860s, the handloom weaver of Lancashire cotton became
rtually extinct.

Many of the new mill masters were originally spinners
weavers who saved or borrowed enough to go into
usiness on a larger scale. Joseph Rylands and his two sons
ere handloom weavers in Wigan and St. Helens before
tting up the Gidlow works. Many became very rich. At
s death in 1841, William Woods was reputedly worth

£300,000, but fortunes were both made and lost within the
town in the early 1800s, and built up Sovereign Mills by
ruthless exploitation of his workforce. He became mayor
of Wigan in 1823, and again in 1830, but shortly
afterwards his businesses collapsed and he died in poverty.

The growing importance of cotton to the economic
prosperity of the town was revealed by the factory
inspectors' returns of 1835. There were nearly 5,000 men
women and children working in twenty one mills at that
time, out of a total population of 11,000. Although cotton

Rylands had their own fire service, so extensive was the site. Here the firemen
e with their hoses shortly before the outbreak of the First World War.

was dominant, there were still eleven linen manufacturers in Wigan in 1824, and a directory of that date lists fustian as a principal fabric. Linen was still being produced as late as 1858, but by the end of the century neither linens nor fustian were being manufactured in the town.

Wigan specialised in the spinning of coarse to middling cotton yarns, which meant that while America, the supplier of cheap raw cotton was embroiled in Civil War in the 1860s, the town was very badly hit. In 1862 only two out of Wigan's thirty five mills were working at full capacity, and almost seven thousand out of a total workforce in the mills of nine thousand were out of work. Woods and Eckersleys spent as much as £3,500 on bread and soup for the operatives they would normally have employed in a four year period up to August 1865. Economic growth does not appear to have been severely handicapped by the by the cotton famine, and a boom followed in the 1870s. From this period the development of the industry was characterised by its concentration in the hands of larger firms. Ring spinning, a more economic method of making yarns, began to replace mule spinning in Wigan mills in the mid 1880s.

Many textiles were woven for making into clothes, and the mass production of clothing became a factory trade in the last quarter of the nineteenth century. In Wigan Timothy Coop set up a factory in 1872 enploying 500 people. This branch of the industry continued to expand and by the 1930s there were as many as 2,000 people employed by a number of firms in the area.

The cotton industry in Wigan continued to prosper throughout the 1890s and by the turn of the century, the development of ever larger textile groups continued. In 1900 Eckersleys became part of the Amalgamated Cotton Mills Co. Ltd. a company with a controlling interest in a considerable number of mills in the North West.

If an expression of confidence in the future of the industry was needed, it was supplied by Woods who built the present Trencherfield Mill in 1908. It had a capacity of 60,000 ring and 24,000 mule spindles and was capable of employing one thousand workers. By 1911 there were nearly eight thousand workers in the industry and six thousand of them were women.

After the First World War the cotton industry appeared to be economically sound. The number of spindles in Wigan mills passed the million mark in 1908 and stayed there until 1934. But these figures hid an

industry which was shrinking rapidly. There were sligh more workers in the mills in 1921 than before the war, b by 1931 two thousand jobs had disappeared. Worsl Mesnes Mill closed in 1926, Lowe Mills in Hindley in 193 by which date all the mills in the area were either on sho time or operating well below their capicity. The indust was being hit by competition from Japan - whose cott industry had built up rapidly and, indeed, had be competing in what were traditionally seen as Briti markets in South East Asia from as early as 1918

In an attempt to defend themselves, a number of mi combined to form the Lancashire Cotton Corporation 1929. The Corporation soon owned one hundred and for mills, including Trencherfield, May Mills in Pembert and Empress Mill in Ince. They installed new machiner and at Trencherfield completed the changeover from mu to ring spinning by 1932, when the mill employed nea 600 workers.

The government intervened in 1936 with the Cott Industry Reorganisation Act, which set up a board to b and scrap surplus capacity. It was the final recognition th the days of Britain supplying the world with cotton we gone. The industry, though, was far from dead, but had compete also with new synthetic fibres developed in t 1950s and 60s. Between 1951 and 1965 employment cotton manufacture in Wigan fell from nearly 11,000 just over 7,000, a loss of some three and a half thousa jobs, although cotton was still the town's main employe

That period also witnessed the beginning of a peri of closures. Rylands closed in 1954, Victoria Mills in 195 and both Enfield and Empress Mills closed in 1975. M Mills finally closed its doors in 1980 and was demolish shortly afterwards.

A textile industry in Wigan still exists - but workforce can now be numbered in hundreds rather th thousands.

John Thomas Beesley with a new loom at Rylands' Gidlow Mills about
20. John Beesley's daughter, Margaret, from whom these pictures
ne, went herself to work at Gidlow Mills in 1923 as a trainee weaver.
e worked with a group of four weavers, spending one quarter of a day
th each. Her jobs initially included sweeping around the looms, and for
keeping the area around sixteen looms clean she earned tuppence. The
overlookers were responsible for setting up the looms, getting faults fix-
ed, changing warps etc. and were paid on the output of the weavers under
their supervision.

13

6. Rylands' Gidlow Mills. Group of overlookers taken about 1906. T
mill manager is in the centre of the picture, with John Beesley sitting
his immediate left. Standing behind the manager is John's brother Alfr
who left Rylands shortly after this picture was taken to become und
manager at Eckersleys Swan Meadow Mills.

, Wigan postcard publisher Will Smith, who had a shop on Wigan Lane,
roduced a series of photographs of Wigan Mill Girls between 1904 and
)10. They were printed by the collotype process by a firm in Germany as
nith believed no British printer could match quality and price. This im-
ge shows part of the Carding Room. Here the impurities were removed
om the cotton and the first stage in a process which resulted in all the
bres of cotton lying parallel was achieved.

WIGAN MILL GIRLS, CARD-ROOM.

8. Another postcard caption as being the card room, this image shows the traditional "uniform" of the mill girl before the Great War.

9. A few paces to the right to the location of the previous picture, but this time captioned as the Drawing Room, the same group of workers posed for another picture - this time with two of the girls holding shuttles.

10. The Drawing Frames showing the drawn cotton in its "cans". The drawing frames further refined the cotton and, depending on the type and quality of yarn ultimately needed, removed the shorter fibres, and blended the cotton drawn from four or more cans into a single coil. This process could be repeated several times until the required quality was achieved.

11. Until the cotton enters the slubbing frame, the thickness of the c[…] and the naturally cohesive qualities of the fibres have been sufficient […] hold them together. Now, however, as the material is thinned out, on[…] the application of a twist will hold the fibres together. In some areas, t[…] slubbing frames were known as the flyer frames, and during this part […] the process the fibre is drawn out to a much thinner and finer gauge a[…] given a much needed twist to hold it together.

WIGAN MILL GIRLS, CARDROOM.

MILL GIRLS, DRAWING-ROOM, N°2.

17

DRAWING FRAMES.

SLUBBING FRAMES.

19

MILL GIRLS, MULE-ROOM, No. 2.

Wigan Mill Girls, Mule Room No2, Rylands Mill. Here the cotton is ally spun. Wigan mills held on to mule spinning long after the faster d more efficent ring spinning system had been adopted widely ewhere. Indeed some Wigan mills did not abandon their mules until the 20s. Trencherfield was constructed for both ring and mule spinning, h the mules finally being replaced in 1923. The principle of the mule in- ved drawing a strand out and twisting it as the frame moved outwards, n winding the spun cotton as the frame returned to rest . With ring nning, the machine, which took up less floor space, drew out the cot- i, and twisted and wound it in a single continuous process.

13. Although captioned as being part of the weaving room, this photograph seems to show part of the winding process preparatory to warping, or beaming as it is known locally.

14

14. In the warping room, the strands of cotton were aligned and wound carefully to make the warps which are the basis of all weaving. Several stages were involved in making a single warp - the output of several beaming machines being combined to produce a single warp.

15. Also in the Beaming Room at Rylands, several hundred individual threads can be seen here being wound together onto a beam.

. Rylands Mill, Weaving Room No1. The noise in the weaving shed was
ch that normal speech was impossible. Mill girls quickly learned to lip
ad and communicate to each other across the floor despite the constant
atter of the shuttles.

. Rylands Mill Weaving Room No2. Here flannelette sheeting, calicos,
d a wide variety of other cotton products were produced.

WIGAN MILL GIRLS, WEAVING - ROOM, No 2.

18. "Aunty Alice Milligan (bottom right) and workmates at Rylands Cotton Mill" taken by Hill & Son, 48 Standishgate, Wigan. about 1908.

19. Also in Rylands Mill, this view of a carding machine was taken shortly before the mill ceased production.

20. The spinning room at Rylands, again shortly before closure.

21. Two Wigan Mill Girls, mill unknown, taken about 1910. The style of dress chosen by the mill girls seems to have conformed to one of two styles - this cotton overdress being the more common at the period. The alternative style - seen in pictures 13, 17 and 19 - consisted of a white pinafore over a nicely styled dark dress.

22. Wigan Mill Girls. In this picture the girls are holding bobbins of cotton. Mill unknown, date about 1910.

23. Eckersleys Mill The Card Room. The huge Eckersleys Mill complex at Swan Meadow came about after the amalgamation of two separate cotton companies - J. Eckersley & Sons Ltd. and ffarington Eckersley & Co. Ltd. and the two companies could trace their origins back at least until the end of the eighteenth century. This photograph and the ones which follow were taken in 1922 when the mills formed part of the Amalgamated Cotton Mills Trust Ltd.

24. Eckersleys Mill. The cotton spinning process was laid out as an almost continuous production line on the huge mill floors.
This picture, described as another veiw of the carding room, actually shows the drawing process, with the ring spinning frames beyond.

29

25. There were six spinning mills on the site at the time these pictures were taken, Swan Meadow Old Mill, Swan Meadow Large Mill, Water Heyes Mill, and Western Mills Nos. 1, 2 and 3. In total they housed 236,572 ring spindles and 14,544 of the older, and more extravagant in space terms, mule spindles.

26. Another veiw of the ring spinning rooms. In the early nineteenth century, Eckersleys spun their yarns and passed them out to hand loom weavers. The hand loom weavers wove the cloth on their own looms - some of their cottages stood of Wigan Lane until less than thirty years ago - and then brought the finished cloth back to the mill.

27. Eckersleys Mill. Winding Department. This picture, from the company's 1923 year book, is captioned as showing "an operative using the Patent Knot Tying Machine".

28. Eckersley's Mill, the Beaming Department. Yarn from the mill was either bundled for sale to other mills, or made up on beams for their own use or customer's use

29. Eckersley's Mill, the Warping Department. The company prided itself that in addition to a huge yarn export trade, and trade with the home market, they were able, themselves, to accept raw baled cotton at one end of the complex and ship out finished cloths at the other.

30. Eckersleys Mill. Patent Warp Drawing Machine. The girls from Eckersleys spent their lunch break 'parading' up and down Wallgate. "The noise of clogs" said one former mill worker, "was deafening, but for two weeks in the summer, Wallgate fell silent."

33

31. Eckersleys Mill, Patent Warp Tying Machine. Before the invention
such a device, the girls had to tie broken ends by hand. This little dev
was both quicker and safer for the operatives. For a more detailed look
the knot tying implememt, see picture No75.

32. Hand packing of special yarns for export, Eckersleys Mill 1922.

31

33. Eckersleys Mill. Making up
and Bundling Warehouse, 1922.

34. Dorma Ltd. Eckersleys Mill.
Beaming Department 1986. Two
high speed beaming machines keep
the looms supplied. Margaret
Johnson is seen here at work on
one of them just before Christmas
1986.

35. Dorma Ltd. Sizing Department. Here several beams are combined to produce a single warp, sufficient to keep a loom working for two weeks round the clock.

36. Dorma Ltd. Weaving Shed. One hundred and eighty looms, now controlled by less than a dozen weavers. The noise is deafening, but ear protectors must be worn nowadays, unlike the turn of the century. Each weaver now looks after about eighteen looms. At the turn of the century, that number would probably have had four or six weavers plus apprentices.

Production from this one shed exceeds 4½ million metres of woven cotton annually

37. Eckersleys Mill, 1942. Mill girls queue up at the canteen for their break. Most of the girls in this picture, unusually for Wigan, are wear shoes. Clogs were common footwear for mill girls well into the 195 "Your clogs were always two sizes too large when you first went into mill' said one former mill girl "so you had to get your money's worth of them."

Eckersleys Mill complex from the air. In the 1920s, the firm enployed
er three thousand people.

Loading raw cotton into a blending machine at Eckersleys Mill, about 50.

Inside Eckersleys Mill. This superb photograph of the ring spinning mes at Eckersleys dates probably from about 1950. The number of ndles in Wigan mills at this time had dropped a little from the peak of er a million between the wars.

41. The first Trencherfield Mill had been opened in 1820, with No2 mill completed between 1851-2. Both had belt driven equipment rather than the rope drives of the third mill. This photograph taken when renovation work was started preparatory to the establishment of the Mill at the Pier shows the boiler house being demolished. The free standing chimney stood in the middle of what is now the main car park.

42. Trencherfield Mill & the Mill at the Pier, 1983. This mill complex c £120,000 to construct and equip between 1906 and 1908. It was built a fireproof spinning mill with 60,000 ring spindles and 24,000 mu. William Woods & Son also owned Sovereign Mills in Scholes, a William himself was originally described as a "putter out of yarns" Wigan's body of home-based hand loom weavers.

43. Five years after the Mill was opened, Woods went into liquidation, and the company was acquired by Alexander Young and renamed Trencherfield Mill Ltd. By the time this picture was taken of the carding machines about 1949-1950, it was part of the Lancashire Cotton Corporation, who acquired it in 1932.

44. Carding Machines at Trencherfield Mill 1950.

45. Trencherfield was always a spinning mill - with a huge card room built as a single storey building in front of the present building. This picture shows the Under-Carder one Saturday morning in 1950.

46. Mixed cotton coming out of the blending machine, Trencherfield M
1950.
47. Ring spinning frames at Trencherfield Mill 1950.

TRENCHERFIELD MILL
WIGAN

THE NEW TRENCHERFIELD MILL.

CHRISTENING THE ENGINES.

WIGAN AS AN INDUSTRIAL CENTRE.

MAYOR ON THE NEGLECTED OPPORTUNITIES OF THE PAST.

he formal opening of the new Trencherfield of William Woods and Son, Ltd., of Wigan, place on Wednesday afternoon, when the cere of christening the engines was gone through, presence of a goodly gathering of share- rs and invited guests interested in local stries. The engines are of the four-cylinder expansion type, made to turn 2,100 indicated power at a speed of 65 revolutions per te, and to work with a boiler pressure of 200lbs. dimensions of the cylinder are, high pressure ches intermediate 40 inches, and the two low- re cylinders 44 inches, the stroke being 5ft power is transmitted to the mill by rope pulleys, in diameter, and grooved for 54 ropes, 1¾in in ness. The engines were made by Messrs. John Edward Wood, engineers, of Bolton. The mill been built on modern lines and is up-to-date ery respect. It will have the advantage of carriage, a special arm of the canal, which s right to the mill having been constructed. eat interest was taken in the proceedings. rman S. Wood, the Mayor of Wigan, wearing hain of office, was present, with the Mayoress, among the gathering were Alderman W. rock, J.P., Alderman J. T. Gee, J.P., Messrs. , Burland, J.P., J. Heaton, J.P., S. Brown, G. Rushton, J.P., O. Rushton, J.P., C. ston, C. V. Howarth (vice-chairman of the Kenneth Marshall (managing director), S. am (secretary), H. C. Darlington, J. Ballard, P. ell, J. F. Simpkin, W. Webster, W. Thornley, rington, W. W. Dewse and Councillor Wat- gh, and others, including a large number of en. Refreshments were served, the caterer s Mr. Whalley, and music was discoursed by s Grime and Son's Band.

THE CHRISTENING CEREMONY.

Howarth, who presided over the ceremony, d each of the ladies, who had been asked to en the engines, to perform their services, ampagne being broken over the industrial

Kenneth Marshall, who was the first lady upon, said she had great pleasure in christen- he engine around which they were gathered he name of "Rina," and in doing so she d every success and prosperity to the con-

O. Rushton christened the second engine en.

Gaskell christened the third engine garet

Sharrock, who christened the electric engine it by the name of "Jean."

S. Wood, the Mayoress, set the engines otion, after the christening ceremony.

S. Graham afterwards switched on the electric

he close of the ceremony, Mr. Howarth pre- d each of the ladies who had taken part in eremony with an interesting souvenir it. the of a pair of silver vases

WIGAN AS AN INDUSTRIAL CENTRE.

Mr. O. Rushton, J.P., said they were all sorry that their chairman, Col. Will Woods, was not able to be present with them on that occasion, on account of being out of the country, but in his absence they had excellent representatives in Mr. Howarth, their vice-chairman, and Mr. Kenneth Marshall their managing director. The name of Marshall was one to be conjured with in the Wigan district. Mr. Kenneth Marshall's father was held in great affection by all in Wigan who had grown up under his influence, and his grandfather was a leading minister at one of their Wigan Noncon- formist churches generations ago. The name of Marshall would long remain in the hearts and memories of the Wigan people. (Hear, hear). They had one of the finest mills in Lancashire, and there was not the slightest doubt about it that it would prove a great success. The old methods of twenty-five or thirty years ago would not do to-day, and they had up-to-date machinery adapted for the twentieth century in their mill. They were all pleased at the presence of the Mayor and Mayoress, and glad that they had taken part in the opening ceremony. He was sure that the Mayor had done his work nobly during his year of office, and they would all be sorry when he had to make way for his successor. He hoped that that cere- mony would be the first stepping stone to the success of the Trencherfield Mill. (Applause.)

THE MAYOR AND WIGAN'S NEGLECTED OPPORTUNITIES

The Mayor said in taking part in those proceed- ings that day he was associating himself with one of the most important functions during his year of office. Wigan was an old town: they always alluded to it as the ancient and loyal borough. But he would like to ask how it got that name. If they cared to consult the records they would find Wigan was a very important community cen- turies ago, when Liverpool and Manchester were unknown practically speaking. One was bound to ask how it was that Wigan having such a magni- ficent start, was to-day standing in the background compared with some of those communities more recently established? Wigan was only looked upon as a Lancashire manufacturing town instead of being a city of industry. He thought the reason was that in the past advantages had not been taken of the opportunities as they ought to have been. They had had enterprising men, but not enough of them. The population to-day was greater than it had ever been before; and he thought they had room enough of enterprise than ever, and he sincerely hoped that that day marked the dawn of a new era of prosperity for Wigan and the neighbourhood. (Hear, hear). Wigan, to his mind, was the centre of south-west Lancashire. Having referred to its position as regards Lancashire, he said they had got railway facilities equal to any other provincial town, and a great deal superior to a great many; had carrying facilities in the way of good canals, which many towns would be pleased to have, and good roads between the principal cities; with all those advantages Wigan ought to go ahead a great deal faster than it was doing. He believed all that was needed was a genuine spirit of enterprise, such as had been manifested in putting up that magnificent mill. That enter- prise, however, should not be confined to a few, but the very inhabitants themselves should feel that they ought to invest their spare money in an enterprise which would find employment for some one else. Andrew Carnegie, in his book called "The Gospel of Wealth," spoke of the very great

pride the first cheque he received as dividend gave him, for it was absolutely the first money that had gone into their family which nobody had worked for. If they could only get the young men and women to exercise the same spirit of enterprise by becoming shareholders in manufactories, thereby taking a greater interest in such undertakings, they would begin to try on all occasions to bring forward something that was good and of importance to the town, finding employment for others and bringing profit to themselves. He hoped the venture of that day would prove a lasting success, that those who had had the courage to put money in that undertaking would never regret it, and that the example set would stimulate others to copy it, with the result that the mill might turn out not only a benefit to the shareholders but increase the prosperity of their dear old town. (Applause.)

Alderman Sharrock said he was proud to be asso- ciated with anything that concerned Wigan. Speak- ing of Wigan as a centre of industry he said that Wigan was a chartered borough when Manchester was a village, and it looked very strange that Manchester to-day had grown into the commercial centre of Lancashire while Wigan had been almost standing still. There was no reason why Wigan should not be the industrial centre of South-West Lancashire, and what they wanted to achieve was more local enterprise. He said that in order that they might enjoy prosperity to the full it was necessary that labour and capital should work together harmoniously for the good of both. At the present time while they were engaged in that ceremony there was a dark cloud hanging over the cotton industry in this country, and he hoped that this would soon pass away. His idea was that there should be proportions in all things and equality as far as possible, so that all men might share the benefits of the world. His advice to the people of Wigan was that they should help forward such local industries as that for which that new mill had been built by investing their money in it, because without the necessary capital work could not be provided as they would like to provide it for the people of the district. (Applause.)

Alderman Gee said that in his opinion there wasn't a handsomer nor a finer mill in Lancashire than the Trencherfield Mill—(hear, hear)—and he congratulated the directors upon their enterprise in putting up that mill. Before long they would be employing in that mill more than 1,000 hands. They heard a great deal about employment and un- employment, and he was not going into the economic discussion of the question of unemployment, but the directors of Messrs. William Woods and Son had been doing what they could to do away with unemployment by erecting that fine mill in connec- tion with the opening ceremony of which they were present on that occasion. There might be a cloud hanging over the industry, but it would soon pass away, and his advice to them was not to be down- hearted by the present transitory conditions of things. He ventured to prophesy that although things looked black, the outlook would be limited to the year 1908, and that before long all the shareholders in that concern would be satisfied with their investments and the whole of the employees with what they were getting in wages. (Applause.)

A vote of thanks was passed to the Mayor and Mayoress for their presence on the motion of Mr. O. Rushton, who said that he taught the Mayor as a boy in the Sunday school, and he naturally thought that something of his Worship's success was due to that teaching. (Laughter and applause.)

The proceedings were terminated with the sing- ing of the National Anthem.

48. Clara Knowles, Beamer, Trencherfield Mill 1950. Very few of the girls knew anything of other parts of the manufacturing process other than their own. If you were a beamer, you knew about beaming and little else. A cheese winder might not know anything of life in the card room. "You weren't trained to think" said one old lady "you were trained to do."

49. The opening of a new cotton mill in the town especially one as sophisticated as Trencherfield - was a significantly newsworthy event. The Wigan Observer carried an extensive report on the opening of the third Trencherfield Mill - the present one - in 1908 by William Woods & Son.

50. The famous Trencherfield Mill Engine, now splendidly restored and running daily as one of the major attractions of the Wigan Pier Heritage Trail.

. Hand loom weaver's cottages, Wigan Lane. These houses, typical of hundreds which housed Wigan's weaving looms in the eighteenth and nineteenth centuries, were on the site now occupied by Swinley Labour Club.

52. May Mills, Pemberton, seen across the nearby churchyard. There [has?] been a mill on this site from the 1860s, when the original May Mill [was] built by Joseph Roper, farmer, colliery proprietor and cotton spinne[r].

53. May Mills shortly before demolition. A second mill had been built in 1890 to replace the original, destroyed by fire in 1884, and this third mill completed twelve years later.

54. High on the gable, the name May Mills and the date 1902 dominated the local skyline. May Mills, being next to Blundells Colliery and the pit's extensive railway sidings was one of only a very few mills in the Wigan area not dependent upon the canal. Coal was delivered at pit head prices, and cotton was delivered and dispatched through those sidings.

55. Inside May Mills, early 1950s. From relatively small beginnings -only 20,000 spindles at the turn of the century, May Mills had over 75,000 by the 1930s. It became part of the Courtaulds Group in the early 1960s, producing carpet fibres until closure in 1980, and demolition very shortly afterwards.

56. May Mill Girls, 1930s. Some of the machinery these girls operated is now in Trencherfield as part of the cotton exhibition the Machinery Hall next to the Mill Engine.

57. May Mill Girls, 1930s. These girls were trained to operate only in one area. If you were training to be a winder, you started off sweeping up. Promotion meant being allowed to fetch and carry bobbins. Eventually they would progress to the skill task itself.

56

58. Mill Girls, Dicconson Lane Mill Aspull, about 1920. Taken on the steps at the mill entrance. The girls in the front row are Bella Brown, Louisa Edwards, Lily Gibson and Lily Rigby. Behind are Maggie Lundy and Nellie & Polly Rigby. Louisa Edwards and her friends were bobbin fillers. They were on piece work getting about two pounds wages on a good week -but if there were no bobbins to fill, there was no work and therefore no pay. Their working conditions were better than in the weaving shed, where girls traditionaly worked in bare feet. Louisa had started work at Rose Bridge Mill straight from school at 13 years of age where she earned four shillings and sixpence a week working from 6a.m. until 5.30p.m. She moved to Dicconson Lane in 1920. The Mill gates there were shut at 7a.m. in the morning. Most of the workforce came from Aspull, and viewed Top Lockers as foreigners. On one occasion the Aspull workers stopped the machines, refusing to work with foreign labour!

59. Mill Girls with 'snap baskets' and cans. This superb study of Wigan Mill girls was taken in the 1890s by the eminent local amateur photographer, the Reverend William Wickham.

60. Group of Wigan Mill Girls with shuttles, mill unknown. This picture was taken probably about 1900. The friendships which developed in the mills - amongst young girls straight from school, often lasted lifetimes. "They were happiest days of our lives in't factory" said one mill girl of her apprenticeship days just after the Second World War, "I'd happily go back tomorrow as a winder."

61. Mule Room, Taylors Mill, Miry Lane, 1937. In this photograph
mill is decorated for the Coronation of King George VI in May 1937
but one of the apprentices are barefoot, the normal practice in many l
mills. Vincent Waring, who loaned this picture, is the lad leaning on
post in the middle row.

Baled yarns on display, Empress Mills Ince, 1930s. The Empress Spin-
; Company became Empress Mill Ltd. in 1920 before becoming first
of the Lancashire Cotton Corporation and then Courtaulds before
ıre in 1975 with the loss of 350 jobs.

63. Mrs. Conner, a beamer at Empress Mills in the 1930s, dressed up at Christmas time. The staff were allowed to wear other than their working clothes at Christmas, and Mrs. Conner is seen here in black dress, black shoes and stockings. The crochet collar of the dress was made while at her work. Several former mills girls talk of using broken ends of cotton to crochet a wide variety of garments and garment decorations while at work. Snoods, small crocheted bands for holding hair in place, seem to have been the most common, although collars and cuffs for dresses, and even shawls and complete bodices do not seem to have been unusual.

64. Local professional photographer James Millard paid homage to Wigan's working women when he built his new photographic studio in Market Street - on the site now occupied by the Queens Hall. An amateur sculptor as well as a photographer, astronomer and telescope maker, he created a pit brow lass for one side of the building, and a mill girl for the other. The sculpture bears the date 1895 in this photograph taken by his son about 1905.

65. Sandbrook Mill Orrell, from the air. The mill was built in 1862
Abraham Peter Widdows, cotton manufacturer of Orrell and Chor
The distinction in the trade directories of being listed as a manufactu
was kept for those mills which has weaving sheds.

Sandbrook Mill Girls, 1937. Having photographs taken to celebrate
onations seems to have been traditional. These girls are posing in the
yard.

67. Spinning Room, Sandbrook
Mill, Orrell, 1937 - again decked
out with flags for the Coronation
of King George VI. Much of the
mill at the time these pictures were
taken had been rebuilt after a
serious fire in the 1880s.

Pennyhurst Mill, Wallgate, c.1908. The original Pennyhurst Mill was
pinning Mill opened in the 1840s, with 40,000 spindles and owned by
n Wood & Co. by the 1860s. The building was almost completely
troyed by fire in 1885 and the company was wound up. On the site rose
ew Pennyhurst Mill used, by the time this picture was taken, for
thing manufacture.

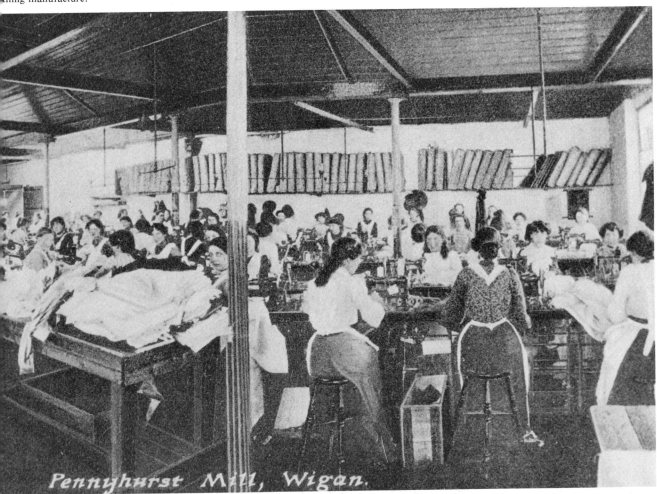

Pennyhurst Mill, Wigan.

69. Shuttle flies out - Put it on't bench. One of a series of cautionary cards aimed at increasing awareness of the dangers of careless working habits in Lancashire cotton mills, produced about 1900.

CUTLOOKER WANT'S TH'I
HELLO! THAT WRONG COP I LET GO

70. Cutlooker wants th'i…Hello! That wrong cop I let go…A turn-of-the-century attempt at quality control. The series of these cards must have been extensive - this is No28.

72. Mill Girl and Apprentice, Unknown Wigan mill about 1900. 71

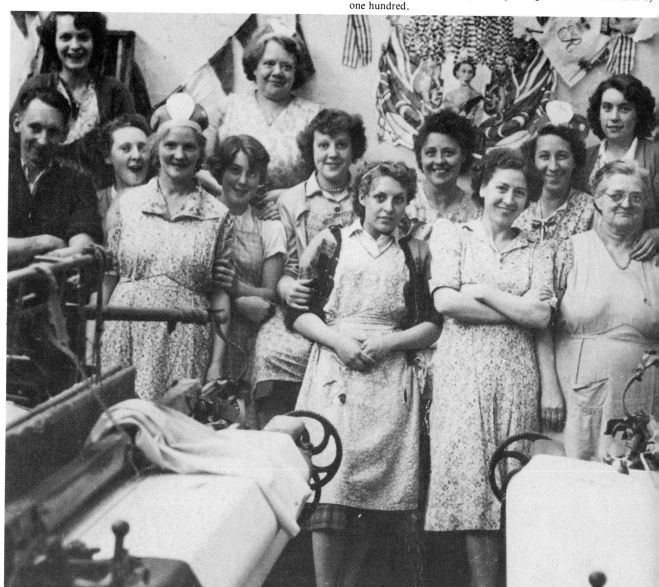

Mill Girls and Overlooker, Enfield Mills, 1953. During the Second
World War production at the mill was turned over to the manufacture of
[ ]h for barrage balloons. The mill eventually closed in 1975, two weeks
[ ]re Christmas.

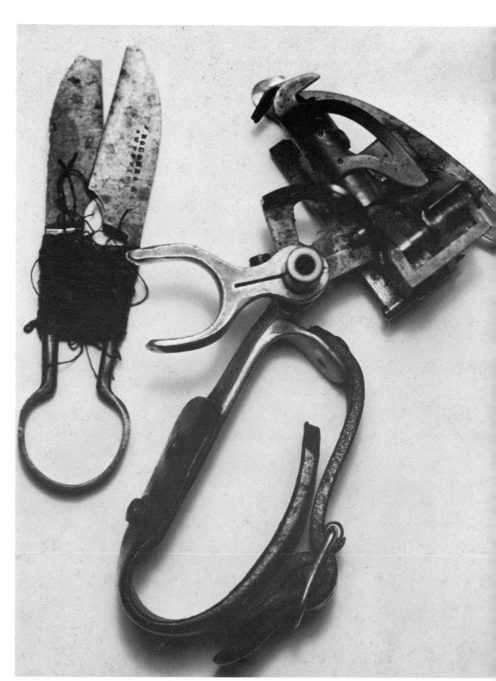

75. Patent Knot tying machine, and knotter's scissors. To see this implement in use, refer back to picture No27.

76. Wigan mill girls, 1910. This photograph, probably taken at Rylands' Gidlow Mills shows the inside of the mill decorated for the Coronation of King George V. At either edge of the picture can be seen the belts which drove the machinery, with the drive shafts running across the full length of the top of the picture.

77. Another veiw taken on the same occasion.

78. Timothy Coop's factory in Dorning Street. Coop was a tailor in Wallgate in the 1860s when he became involved in trying to solve the problems which beset the Lancashire coal and cotton industries during the American Civil War. After a visit to America he was convinced that the future for clothing manufacture lay in large factories rather than small one or two-man businesses. With his partner James Marsden he decided to train local girls to use sewing machines and manufacture mens clothing. The result of this enterprise grew into this large purpose built factory opened in 1872.

79. Coop's factory from the air.

80. An early advertisement for Coop's clothing dating from the 1870s.

81. Coop's gentlemen's outfits from an 1887 advertisement.

82. Two wings were added to the factory between 1888 and 1890, and
the time this picture was taken in the early 1950s, Coops were manuf
turing on a vast scale.

Still a major employer in the town, and now part of the Dunn group, photograph shows the production floor of Coop's factory just before Christmas 1986.

84. Wigan mill girls on their way to work, c1950. The girls appear to be walking down Wallgate, on their way, probably to either Eckersleys Mill or to Trencherfield.

85. Going home, c1950. The industry which had given so much work to many people was on borrowed time from the end of the Second World War. By the mid 1960s, closures were becoming commonplace, and by the end of the 1970s, most of the mills had not only closed, but had been razed to the ground.

84

Appendix

...me Trade Directory entries from 1816

...tton Manufacturers

...ton, John, Standishgate
...bler & Ackersley, Millgate
...pleton, Roger, Scholes
...pleton, Peter, Hindley
...hton, Thomas, Millgate
...hworth, Robert, Wiend
...ch, Thomas, Standishgate
...chall, Richard, Aspull
...own, William, Standishgate
...rtwright, John, Bishopgate
...oper, John, Standishgate
...ughtrie, Thomas, Millgate
...upe & Smith, Millgate
...upe, William, Standishgate
...well, Thomas, Wallgate
...rwell, Thomas. Millgate
...rwell, Thomas, Pepper Mill
...tchfield, Peter, Hindley
...ckworth, Joseph, Hardybutts
...ckworth, Richard, Scholes
...cles, William, King Street
...irclough, Joseph, Ince
...skell, George, Wallgate
...een, Thomas, Wallgate
...eenough, John, Wallgate
...eenough, Peter & Sons, Standishgate
...lliwell, William, Standishgate
...rdman, Thomas, Wallgate
...dgson, Cardwell & Kearsley, Standishgate
...llingsworth, Kerr & Co. Wallgate
...pwood & Son, Wallgate
...rrocks, Milner & Co., Wallgate
...hnson, William, Wigan Lane

Kearsley, Thomas, Wigan Lane
Lewis J & E Co., Chapel Lane
Locke, Hindley & Co., Standishgate
Lowe, James, Standishgate
Lowes & Ashton, Scholes
McClare & Wood, Standishgate
Newsham & Burrows, King Street
Peel, Sir Robert & Co., Market Place
Pinnington, Joseph, Hindley
Pooley, Henry, Millgate
Prescot, John snr., Hallgate
Ransome, John, Millgate
Rowe, Henry, Scholes
Turner, Richard, Millgate
Turton & Bingham, Millgate
Woods, William, Wallgate
Worthington, William, Hallgate

Linen & Check Manufacturers

Ashworth, Robert, Wiend
Butterworth, John, Wallgate
Cartwright, John, Bishopgate
Coughtrie, Thomas, Millgate
Cowell, Thomas, Millgate
Fairclough, Charles, Bishopgate
Gaskell, Hugh, Wallgate
Greenough, John, Wallgate
Greenough, Peter & Sons, Standishgate & Up Holland
Hardman, Thomas, Wallgate
Hodson, Cardwell & Kearsley, Standishgate
Hopwood, John & Son, Wallgate
Low & Ashton, Scholes
Prescot, John snr., Hallgate
Rylands, Joseph, Wallgate & St. Helens
Scott, John, Millgate
Worthington, William, Hallgate

Dyers

Appleton, Peter, Hindley
Bullock, John, Millgate
Fogg, John, Queen Street
Grindin, Stephen, Standishgate
Heywood, John, Millgate
Holland, Thomas, Chapel Lane
Lowe, Thomas, Scholes
Naylor, William, Millgate
Waddington, Jonathan, Scholes

Fustian Manufacturers

Ackersley & Ambler, Hindley
Lowe, James, Standishgate
Newsham & Burrows, King Street
Turton & Bingham, Millgate
Tyrer, Hugh, Hindley
Waddington, Jonathan, Scholes

Shuttle Makers

Bibbs, Thomas, Scholes
Molyneux, Isaac, Scholes
Rothwell, James, Market Street

Sizers

Bullock, John, Millgate
Coupe, Thomas, New Church Street
Grindin, Stephen, Wigan Lane
Walker, Thomas jnr., Wigan Lane

Worsted Manufacturers

Harrison, Nathanial, Standishgate

Worrall's Trade Directory 1869

Cotton Spinners

Ashton, James, cotton spinner & grocer, Ashton
Brown, William, Worsley Mesnes
Cross, Joseph, Gidlow Lane
Eccles, Richard, School Common Lane
Eckersley, James & Sons, Swan Meadow Road
Gidlow, James, Newhall Mill, Ince
Harrison & Hopwood, Britannia Mills, Wallgate
Hindley Twist Company, Low Mill, Hindley
Hilton, Thomas, Ellesmere Mills, Newtown

Johnson, William, Wood Street & Bradford Place M
Kilpatrick, Thomas, cotton spinner & doubler, Hin
Green & Tyldesley
Lea, John & Sons, Rose Bridge Mills, Ince
Leigh Brothers, Aspull
Lord, Abraham & Co., cotton spinners & manufactur
Victoria Mills, Platt Bridge
Moore & Lamb, cotton spinners & colliery own
Sovereign Mills
Pennington, Alfred, cotton spinner & manufactu
Worthington Mills Hindley
Roper & Marsden, May Mills, Pemberton
Rylands & Sons, Gidlow Works
Strickland & Walmsley, Water Heyes
Taylor, Thomas & Bros., Victoria Mills, Wallgate
Tipping, William, Chapel Lane
Weedall, T. B. & Co., Chapel Lane Mills
Wilde Brothers, Highfield Mills Pemberton
Wood, John & Co., Pennyhurst Mill, Miry Lane
Woods, William & Sons, Trencherfield Mill

Cotton Manufacturers

Daniel & Green, gingham & cotton manufacturer, Prin
Street
Henry, George, Hindley
Leach, JC & F & Co., gingham & cotton manufacturer
Standishgate
Leigh, Ralph, checks & cotton manufacturer, 28 Whe
Peck, Son & Co., Weir Bridge Mill
Smith, James, Scholes Bridge Mill
Widdows, Alfred P, Orrell

Bobbin Turners

Riddlesworth, John, Queen Street Saw Mills
Wall, Charles, Hindley

Spindle & Fly Makers

Lathom, Ann, Scholes Bridge
Talbot, William, Shaw's Yard, Scholes

Dyers

Cookson, William, Harrogate Street
Corf, John, 45 Millgate
Glencross, Elias, 30 Millgate
Lowe, Thomas, 12 Queen Street